A Concise Book on Hummingbirds

A guide on hummingbirds' species, behavior, feeding, and how to attract hummers in your backyard for beginners

April .k. Brown

Copyright

Table of Content

Chapter One

Hummingbirds

Hummingbirds are the smallest of birds that belong to Trochilidae's avian family, and their closest relatives are the similarly fascinating swifts.

Hummingbirds are tiny (weighing 2 to 20 grams), with most species measuring 7.5-13 cm (three to five inches) lengthwise. They possess long, narrow bills and small, saber-like wings. Hummingbirds got its name from the humming sound they made by beating their wings, thereby flapping it at a high frequency audible to humans.

One of the predominant characteristics of males and female hummingbirds is the colorful small, stiff, highly reflective, colored feathers on the upper chest and throat. These shiny feathers and others around the head at times look sooty black. But the real beauty comes when a hummingbird, while trying to catch the sun, turns its head; this singular act displays the intense, metallic spectral color.

Most male hummingbirds found in California have flashy throat patches called gorgets. Females and young birds don't have any throat patches and have duller, greenish-grey feathers except for female Allen's and Rufous hummingbirds – which possesses some coppery-orange color.

Chapter Two

Types of Hummingbirds

There are about 356 species of hummingbirds recorded in the world. That's quite a number, and 51 out of 356 hummingbirds are endangered species.

Common species of hummingbirds

1. Allen's Hummingbird

Scientific Name: Selasphorus Sasin

Summer Habitat: Central Mexico

Winter Habitat: California/Oregon south to Los Angeles
United States

Allen's hummingbirds are year-round residents on the Palos
Verdes Peninsula.

Allen's hummingbirds are occasionally mistaken for Rufous
hummingbirds because of their similar orange plumage.
Allen's can be identified by much greener back while the
Rufous Hummingbird has a coppery back. Allen's
hummingbirds also have more extensive orange on the
flanks. The male Allen's has a throat that shows different
colors from orange-red to yellow-orange, a greener back, and
a Rufous rump and tail feathers. The Females Allen can
appear as identical as a rufous hummingbird.

Allen's hummingbirds can be found in suburban gardens and
open woods. They come to the nectar feeder regularly in
early spring because of their early migration.

2. Anna's Hummingbird

Scientific Name: Calypte Anna

Summer Habitat: The United States along Alaska,
Washington, Oregon, California, and the Southern States.
Western Canada. Winter Habitat: Southern United States,
Mexico

This hummingbird is the most common along the Pacific
coast. It has year-round residents.

The male, when moving from flower to flower, produces a high-pitched, loud popping sound, sounding like a sharp cheep cheep cheep cheep with their tail feathers.

Anna's species is one of the larger and the most vocal hummingbirds in the United States than all other hummingbirds in the United States. All other species of hummingbirds found in the United States are mostly silent.

Anna's species produce a chirping sound with their tail feathers while making a courtship dance. During the courtship dance, the male Anna will fly up to 130 feet in the sky and dive to Earth with a frightening speed before leaping back up to the sky again. One of their territorial behaviors is that the male makes elaborate dive spectacles at other birds.

Males Anna has glossy dark rose-red crowns and throat, which may appear black or dark purple under low light. The back appears metallic green, and underneath is mostly greyish.

Females Anna's have light grey chests with white and red spotting on the throat, greenish back, and white-tipped tails.

They look like Costa's Hummingbirds, but the male's Costa's Hummingbird's throat feathers are longer than that of the Anna's. Anna's are larger than the Rufous Hummingbirds and does not have the rusty coloration like Rufous Hummingbirds.

3.   Name: Berylline Hummingbird

Scientific Name: Amazilia Beryllina

Summer Habitat: Rarely seen in the mountains
Chiricahua of southeast Arizona, Southern United States

Winter Habitat: they are found on forested slopes of
mountains, adjacent brushy areas, and lower slopes in
Mexico, Central Honduras, and Central America.

Berylline is a medium-sized hummingbird that is easily seen
in the highlands and foothills habitats, including pine-oak and
oak forests, scrub, forest edges, thorn forests, clearings with
trees, and suburban gardens.

The Berylline Hummingbird got its name after the sea-green gem beryl. The dominant color of the bird closely bears a resemblance to the color of the gem beryl.

Adult male feathers are emerald green all over, with purple on the rump and some tail feathers and wings. The gorget (throat feathers) has a brighter green color when compared to the back. Adult female features are Similar to the male.

Together with other hummingbirds, Berylline Hummingbirds often gather on the tops of flowering trees to demonstrate their supremacy.

4. Black-Chinned Hummingbird

Male   Female

Scientific Name: Archilochus Alexandri

Summer Habitat: They are found throughout the
mountainous west of eastern Washington and Oregon to
Idaho and as far south as southwestern Texas in the United
States, northern Mexico, and southern British Columbia

Winter Habitat: All-year-round residents in Mexico.

Males black-chinned have purple-and-black shimmering
gorget (throat feathers)that most often appear black, greenish

upper parts, and pale feathers below that form a collar, discolored whitish belly, and dark tail.

Females have green color at the back, dull metallic green above and below are whitish, pale, without buffy-orange tones.

The female and immature male black-chinned hummingbirds look almost alike, and when perched, often show a pale color.

Black-chinned has a habit of pumping its tail more than other hummingbirds.

Adult male occasionally perches on a twig to survey area and chase off intruders.

5. Blue-Throated hummingbird

Scientific Name: Lampornis Clemenciae

Summer Habitat: They can be found primarily in
moist canyons in the Border Mountains of Arizona, New
Mexico, and Texas.

Winter Habitat: Mexico

They are at the top of the feeding hierarchy because of their
aggressive behavior and large size.

The Blue-throated Hummingbird is the largest hummer breeding north of the Mexican border and the United States.

They are always seen at the feeders and flower patches.

The blue-throated hummingbird upper plumage is dull green, diminishing to a moderate grey on the underneath. It possesses white stripes behind the eyes and a narrower stripe projecting backward from the side of its relatively short bill, and to a blackish cheek patch.

The male can be identified by the shimmering blue throat patch (gorget), a white stripe behind and below the eye, which may appear black or grey color in poor light.

The female and young have grey throats.

6. Broad-Billed Hummingbird

Scientific Name: Cynanthus Latirostris

Summer Habitat: the Southwestern United States, including Arizona, New Mexico, to Southwestern Mexico.

Winter Habitat: the Southwestern United States including Texas, Louisiana, but a few vagrants migrates as far north as Wisconsin.

The male (northern) is glossy green above and on the belly area. He has a deep blue throat. His straight and slender bill is vivid red with a black tip, which distinguished them from other U.S. hummingbirds. His slightly notched tail is dark above, and the under tail feathers are white.

The male (Doubleday's) has glittering blue underpants and black under tail coverts.

The broad female bill is less colorful than the male. Her throat feathers, chest, and belly are light to moderate grey. The base of the bill is broad. There is presence of a white stripe over each eye.

7. Broad-Tailed Hummingbird

Scientific Name: Selasphorus Platycercus

Summer Habitat: Western United States, Central
Mexico, Guatemala

Winter Habitat: Central Mexico, Guatemala, and at times El
Salvador. They migrate through the east of California and
nest in mountain forests and meadows of central California.

Male's features are rose-red throats feathers, white breast, metallic green back and crown, buffy flanks, and broader tails.

Females are mostly pale underneath and lack the flashy throat patch of the male. They have green spots on their throat feathers and cheeks. Their white-tipped outer tail feathers close to the body are rust-colored, and the center tail feathers range from green to blackish.

8. Buff-Bellied Hummingbird

Scientific Name: Amazilia yucatanensis

Summer Habitat: Southern Texas in the United States, the Yucatán Peninsula of eastern Mexico, Belize, Guatemala

Winter Habitat: Gulf Coast of Texas to Florida in the United States. They are usually found in varieties of shrubby or wooded habitats.

The adult male Bluff-bellied has a metallic golden green coloration on the back and crown. The sides are rusty in color, and it also has a cinnamon-buff belly. The tail and main wings are slightly forked and have a rufous color. The bird has a buffy patch on the belly, a very slender red bill with a dark tip, orange tail, and white underwings. It also has an outstanding white lining that is around its eyes. They are always seen at the hummingbirds' feeders.

The female Buff-bellied look almost like the male, although the upper bill is less dark and possesses an outstanding colorful plumage.

9. Costa's Hummingbird

Scientific Name: Calypte Costae

Summer Habitat: Southwestern Arizona in the United
States and the Baja California Peninsula of Mexico

Winter Habitat:: They can be found in Mojave deserts,
deserts shrub, sage scrub area, and thicket in coastal
California, United States, and the Baja California Peninsula of
Mexico.

Adult male Costa Hummingbirds have distinctive bright purple or pinkish crown and gorget (throat patches). The gorget flares out into sharp points at the sides of the throat, giving it an elongated "mustache" appearance. The back and vest are metallic green.

Females have green upperparts with a white eyebrow stripe and whitish underparts like the male except for some black spotting on her throat. The sides of their wings are slightly green. Her tail is dark with white tips on the outer tail plumages.

They look like Anna's Hummingbirds, except the male's gorget (throat feathers) is longer than Anna's.

10. Rufous Hummingbird

Scientific Name (Selasphorus Rufus)

Summer habitat: Arrive in their breeding territory in California up to south-central Alaska, Washington, Oregon, Idaho, and British Columbia.

Winter Habitat: found east of the Mississippi, Northern America., Central America, and Mexico.

Adult males are almost entirely orange plumage with a bright white chest, and some patches of green on the back Throat are iridescent; the color can look anywhere from orange to red through yellow to lime green depending on the light.

Females have whitish, speckled throats, greenbacks and crowns, and rufous, white-tipped tail feathers.

Females are greenish on their upperparts with rusty washed flanks bordering a white chest and abdomen, rusty patches on their green tail Females also have spotting on the throat.

These species of hummingbirds are usually seen in gardens and at feeders.

11. Magnificent Hummingbird

Scientific Name: Eugenes Fulgens

Summer Habitat: Found in southeastern Arizona, southwestern New Mexico in the United States to western Panama and sometimes seen in western Texas.

Winter Habitat:: Found in the southwestern United States to western Panama.

They are one of the largest hummingbird species found in Northern America. Their size can easily identify them.

Overall, the male has a dark green body, a black chest and belly, metallic green gorgets (throat feathers), or brighter blue gorgets when hits by the light. The head appears black with an iridescent purple crown.

The female plumage is plainer with a bright green back and crown. The female underparts are solid grey, and tail feathers tipped with pearl-grey.

12. Ruby-Throated Hummingbird

Scientific Name: Archilochus Colubris

Summer Habitat: Eastern North America and the Canadian grasslands

Winter Habitat: Southern Mexico, Central America as far south as West Indies and Costa Rica.

The ruby-throated hummingbird is mostly seen in the east of North America.

The male has an iridescent ruby-red gorget, a white-collar on the throat, a green crown, an emerald a greenback, and a forked tail.

The female has green upperparts and tail feathers that are banded white, grey-green, and black.

13. Violet-Crowned Hummingbird

Scientific Name: Amazilia Violiceps

Summer Habitat: Breed in Southeastern Arizona in the United States and the southwestern corner of Mexico

Winter Habitat: Southernmost California to southwest Texas. The birds are relatively rare in the United States.

This hummingbird is most easily identified by its distinctive white underparts plumage, plain white throat, iridescent blue-purple (violet) crown, and emerald greenback. The straight and slender bill is red with a black tip.

Male and female birds look almost alike; however, females'
plumages are slightly duller than males. Moreover, the female
has a greener and slightly less brilliant crown.

14. White-Eared Hummingbird

Scientific Name: Hylocharis Basilinna Leucotis

Summer Habitat: Southeastern Arizona, Western Texas,
Florida, Michigan, Mississippi in United States, Northern
Mexico

Winter Habitat: Southeastern Arizona in the United States, Southern Mexico, Nicaragua

White-eared hummingbirds are rightly named because of the broad white ear stripe on both males and females.

Males have a darker body with green plumage and a blue throat, while females have green upperparts and paler whitish-gray underparts.

Male and female white-eared hummingbird's possesses a strongly bicolored bill that is red with a black tip, but males' bills are redder in color.

Both genders also have dark tails; the male's tails are forked in shape while females' tails are straight.

Adult male: Emerald greenback and breast, purple crown, iridescent blue-green chin, prominent white ear stripe, red bill with black tip.

Adult female: Greenback and crown, white breast and sides with green streaks, prominent white ear stripe, red bill with black tip.

15. Green Violet-Ear

Scientific name: Colibri thalassinus

Summer Habitat: Southern Texas, Eastern, and the Central United States and as far north as Ontario.

Winter Habitat: Southern California, Kentucky, Alabama, Texas, Southern Arizona, Missouri, Florida, and Georgia.

In northern America, they live in a semi-open upland country with scrubs and trees.

The hummingbird has an overall iridescent green appearance with a blue or violet ear patch. The chest also has patches of violet. They have dark wings, a blue-green tail, and a bill slightly curved downward.

Females colors and marking are similar but duller when compare to the male.

Chapter Three

Hummingbirds' behavior

1. Social order

Hummingbirds live a very solitary life even; though you may see some sharing a feeder, they do so grudging to grab quick food. They are not very social; hardly travel or migrate together, only come together if they want to mate. They are in their world doing it individually.

Hummingbirds are very territorial and divide themselves by territories. They live in the area they have claimed for themselves based on the abundance of food, water, and nectar. Male hummingbirds can claim about a quarter acre and will aggressively protect it. Females get their territories by the nests they build and staying close to it. Both hummingbirds (male and female) will protect their territory fiercely, but the male is the most aggressive in keeping intruding hummingbirds away.

2. Aggression

Male hummingbirds are very aggressive at the feeder while females' aggressions come alive near their nests. This attitude is interesting and amazing to watch. With the territory already set, the male hummingbirds will chase off any male that flew near. Wading off male intruder helps the male hummingbirds reduce or eliminate the female hummingbirds' competition in that vicinity.

Female hummingbirds always resist male hummingbirds coming close to the nest because the male hummingbird's bright colors attract predators that might be dangerous to the nests' occupants. Most hummingbirds' species display anger and aggression to some extent, but the Rufous hummingbirds have the highest temper.

In late spring or early summer, hummingbirds' aggressive behavior is normally high because they claim territory and guard nests.

When fighting, Hummingbirds are known to body slam each other in midair; at times, they will go as far as locking their bills together, spin in a circle, and eventually hit the ground.

Their aggressive behaviors always result in a fight, and when they fight, they may lose a feather or two. This is hummingbird's war.

Hummingbirds can also show aggression in some other ways like:

a)   Making a loud, fast-paced chirping sound to get an intruder's attention, informing them to stay clear off the already claimed territory.

b) Hummingbirds discourage s an intruder by showing off their size, posture, and strength. A male hummingbird may discourage an intruder by spreading his gorget to display its colors more brightly as a sign of strength. They can also discourage unwelcome guests by pointing the bill at the intruder like a danger, raising and spreading the wings, and flaring the tail.

c) The angry hummingbird warns the intruder to stay away from its territory by diving closely straight down right at the intruder. The intruder, in these cases, maybe an animal or a human being.

d) A dominant hummingbird's chase away intruder by first confronting the intruder at a feeding site, charge at them and chase them off from the flowerbeds or feeder. Angry chirps and other sounds always follow the chase.

e) The last resort hummingbirds show aggression is through fighting, and this discourages intruders from invading their territory. Fighting is an everyday issue for a hummingbird to secure their territory. They fight using their needle-like bills and sharp claws as weapons, which sometimes result in injury or even death.

Solution/curbing

a) Introducing more hummingbirds' feeders help reduces aggression/fighting between hummingbirds, and it encourages more hummingbirds to come to the feeding area. Adding multiple feeders and hummingbirds flower to the feeding area helps the birds to feed without arguing.

b) Make sure you move hummingbird's feeders farther apart from each other to reduce aggression some hummingbirds display while feeding and defending their territory. Hummingbirds are not comfortable feeding side by side. The dominant male always feels threatened whenever hummingbirds are feeding right next to him. Give them some privacy and spread that feeder, or you can buy a feeder with large flowers; the flowers will block their view when they perch to feed.

c)   know what is happening in your area and remove possible aggression causes like hummingbird's predator, feral cat, or another bird. Eliminating the intruder mentioned above when seen around the feeder can help the hummingbirds to calm down

Cleanliness/Grooming

Hummingbirds are big fans of baths and will groom themselves quite often. They use their claws and bills to tidy themselves. The oil gland is located on their back, very close to their tail. They use this oil to cover their wings by using their beak to keep them clean. In places they find it difficult to reach, they will rub themselves against small twigs to assist in cleaning and spreading oils.

They will also use a branch to remove any pollen and debris off their beak. Anytime hummingbirds groom themselves, they swipe their beak back and forth against a branch as if they are sharpening a knife on a knife sharpener.

Hummingbirds like a birdbath and will often fly through misting water, rub themselves against wet leaves after rain, or play in fountains to clean their bodies.

Hummingbirds bath by fluttering their tail and wings in the water, splashing the water on their entire body. After their bath, a hummingbird will meticulously preen each feather until they are dry. Hummingbirds like drying themselves in the sun after a water bath. They do that by fluffing their feather, making sure each nook is free of moisture, and soaking up as much sun as possible.

Baby humming is not left out in this business of grooming. They use the bathroom over the edge of the nest so that it will not mess up the nest.

Courtship/Mating

When male hummingbirds want to inform the females within his territory that he is ready to breed, he will first puff out his chest and throat to display his stunning feathers. Secondly, he will toss his head from one side to the other to flash his feathers in the light, offering the females a little showmanship.

Some will engage in a courtship dive; they fly high into the air and then make a straight dive towards the ground.

They will whistle or make a sound as they are dropping to get the attention of their would-be mate. Before getting to the potential mate down a flight, he will arc his flight straight up, and the process continues. This amazing display will signal the female that he is ready for mating and to the male counterpart to stay clear of his territory.

Male hummingbirds might also do a little mating dance in front of the female hummingbird to get their attention. The dance is done in such a way that it will expose parts of his body, and he will fly rapidly back and forth in front of the female to prove his strength and control. This technique displays how colorful he is to draw the attention of the female.

When female hummingbirds are ready to mate, she will fan her tail feather with a sly look in her eyes and perch on the tree. This shows that she has accepted a partner, and the mating begins.

Chapter Four

Tips for Feeding Hummingbirds

Feeding hummingbirds is an easy task that requires a little effort and knowledge to keep the hummers healthy.. Hummingbirds have voracious appetites, which made them feed six to eight times per hour. To attract hummingbirds in your yard, you need to constantly fill the feeder with nectar. The following are some important information and tips on how to attract and feed hummingbirds.

- **Provide Natural Food Sources like flowers**

Nectar-producing flowers are a major source of food for hummingbirds and rich in nutrients.

Colorful blooming flowers attract hummingbirds. Examples of flowers that hungry hummingbirds feed on are:

Azaleas (Rhododendron spp), foxglove (Penstemon spp), bee balm (Monarda spp), columbines (Aquilegia spp.), cardinal flower (Lobelia spp.), coral bells (Huecheura spp), sage (Salvia spp.), Jewelweed (Impatiens spp), and trumpet creeper.

Hummingbirds also eat gnats, spiders, tree sap, fruit juices, aphids, and other small insects that live on flowers and among the plants.

The hummingbird-friendly flowering plants may vary according to your region, soil, or climate.

- ## Provide Hummingbird Nectar

Hummingbird feeders are designed to provide nectar to hummingbirds like a tubular flower. A simple sugar water solution is poured inside the feeder. The nectar recipes attract hummingbirds the same way as natural nectar sources. A feeder produces a finite amount of nectar each day, unlike a single flower.

A feeder supplies dozens of hummingbirds with enough sugar water every day.

Consider the following when purchasing a hummingbird feeder.

- Choose a feeder with bright red parts; bright colors attract hummingbirds.

- Choose feeders that are simple for easy cleaning and filling.

- Your choice of feeder should have a nectar capacity that matches your size of feeding.

- A feeder should be moderate in size to avoid running out of nectar (small feeder) or nectar becoming bad (very big nectar).

- **Provide more different feeders**

Hummingbird feeders come in different shapes and sizes. If you want to attract more hummingbirds, hang, or spread different feeders in your garden or backyard.

Some hummingbirds have their like and dislike when it comes to choosing feeders. Provide either plastic and glass feeders with multiple access points or just one feeding port.

In your choice of feeder, also consider feeders with and without perches.

- **Placement of feeder**

It is advisable to place your hummingbird feeders where the birds can easily see them and also where you can see and access them without difficulty.

Hang feeders out of direct sunlight and in an area free from breezes to keep the nectar from growing mold, fresh and safe. Placing feeders in a shaded area help distract bees from finding it because wasps and bees love feeding in direct sunlight.

For hummingbirds to get easy access to feeders, hang your feeders very close to nectar-producing flowers or close to any bright decoration in your yard especially, red.

- **Keep the Insects away.**

Provide feeders with built-in insect traps or guards to prevent bees, wasps, and ants from entering.

Feeders that have yellow ports or decorations should be avoided because yellow color attracts wasps and bees.

Avoid the use of sticky products or oil on the feeder's pole; birds feathers can stick on these products and preening might become difficult.

Keep away from toxic insecticides, which can also contaminate feeders and become deadly to the birds.

- **Fill feeders moderately**

Hummingbird's nectar easily ferments in hot weather, so avoid filling feeders with more nectar than the birds can consume in a day. Nectar should be change regularly even if your hummingbirds have not consumed all.

If you fail to change the nectar regularly, the spoiled nectar (sugar solution) can cause the birds to grow a fungus on their tongues. The fungus will make eating difficult, thereby causing starvation, which leads to the death of the hummers.

Always keep your feeder moderately filled.

- **Keep your feeder clean.**

For best results, clean your hummingbird feeder at least two to three times per week with vinegar or bleach solution and hot water. Clean all the nooks and crannies to remove all molds, old nectar, fungus, or crystallized sugar.

The feeder should be clean immediately after you change the nectar. Please avoid using soap to clean your hummingbird's feeders.

- **Provide Migration Meals**

Hummingbirds migrate during late fall and early spring. Because of their migration pattern, they need energy, which means more food to embark on this journey. The extra meals give the hummingbirds energy for their long flights. To attract the first returning hummingbird after migration, place clean and filled feeders early the next spring.

Signs of bad nectar

Hummingbird's feeders need regular cleaning and filling if you want to attract more healthy hummers to your yard. Hummingbird's nectar can spoil as easily as other bird's food, so be careful not to put hummingbirds at risk with spoilt nectar.

Below are some of the tips to tell if your hummingbird's nectar is bad and needs replacement.

Bad nectar

- Hummingbird nectar is a combination of sugar and water when made new. As it gets older, it changes to something different because the sugars break down into other carbohydrates and become less nutritious and digestible for hummingbirds. Spoilt nectar grows fungus, mold, and bacteria, which can be dangerous to hummingbirds.
Fermented nectar gives out a strong odor that attracts insects, raccoons, rats, or even bears, and these pests a great danger to hummingbirds.
Another effect of fermented nectar on hummers is that it coats the bills and feathers of feeding hummingbirds, making it difficult for birds to feed or sip.
When the nectar is fresh, it flows freely through the feeder, and the hummers can eat easily.
Signs of Spoilage

- Fresh nectar is always clear and transparent, just like clean water. For clear indication, always keep your nectar dye-free.

- Spoiled, bad, or rancid nectar may show milky or cloudy discoloration, black or white floating specks.

- Fungus or mold may appear to grow inside the feeder or around the feeding points.

- The presence of floating dead insects inside the feeder's reservoir and some insects might be stuck around the feeding ports.

- Presence of crystallized or sticky residue around the feeding ports, especially for upside-down feeders.

- The hummingbird will stop drinking the nectar, and visiting will also reduce. If you observe that hummingbirds hardly visit a feeder, the best thing is to check the nectar for freshness and replace it immediately.

Steps on how to keep nectar fresh

Nectar gradually spoils as sugar solution breakdown over time, which may endanger the life of hummingbirds. To keep the nectar fresh and healthy for hummers, and ensure less nectar is wasted, take the following steps.

- In choosing your feeder, use hummingbird feeders that will contain less nectar. It will ensure hummingbirds drink most of the nectar before it has a chance to ferment. The feeders will need to be refilled frequently with nectar, and the method won't give room for nectar fermentation.

- Make only nectar quantities that are needed to refill feeders. Don't make extra; if larger quantities are made, keep the unused nectar in the fridge for up to 8-10 days to keep it fresh before usage.

- Place hummingbird feeders out of direct sunlight in shaded, cooler areas. This process prevents faster fermentation and spoilage.

- Ensure you clean and sterilize nectar feeders before each refill to prevent contamination from the previous nectar.

- While cleaning, make sure every nooks and cranny of a feeder is touch because a small amount of leftover food can spoil the whole new nectar.

Use every technique to keep nectar as fresh as possible; the longer the nectar lasts, the better for the birds.

Consider Natural Sources

Another way to feed hummingbirds' fresh, delicious nectar devoid of spoilage or fermentation is to provide them with natural food sources. Nectar-rich flowers naturally replenish and refill their nectar reservoirs and give room for fermentation.

If you want to attract beautiful hummingbirds, start a
hummingbird garden filled with nutritious, colorful blooms
and positions a feeder near it.

Chapter Five

Conclusion

How to Attract More Hummingbirds to Your Feeders

You can attract a greater number of hummingbirds to your garden by following the tactics below.

1. **Introduce a native plant species to your garden:**

Native plants work best instead of exotic species from Asia. The native plant does not only supply nectar to hummingbirds; it also attracts arthropods and insects, making a considerable portion of their diet.

2. **Choose plant species with a different blooming period.**

Plan a continuous blooming schedule by choosing a plant species with different blooming stages; this will provide hummingbirds with food throughout the season. Continuous blooming attracts more hummingbirds to your yard during spring and summer. For example, in the early summer, Fuschia flower bloom, Salvia species do well in mid-summer, and trumpet creeper is an excellent flower for late summer.

Plant different colors of flowers

Red color attracts hummingbirds the most, but they also visit other colors. Don't be afraid to experiments with other colors in your yard.

Alternatively, you can attract a hummingbird by adding a collection of red painted furniture, gazing balls, and other accents to your yard.

3. Provide multiple Feeders.

Using multiple feeders give hummingbirds enough space to feed and also provide an opportunity for more hummers to take a sip. The feeders can be combined in groups and positioned in different feeding stations throughout the yards.

4. Provide larger feeders

Hummingbird's feeders come in different shapes, sizes, and styles. Big feeders with big reservoirs and multiples feeding ports give room for more hummingbirds to feed at once.

5.   Replace old feeders with new ones

If you noticed that the red parts on your hummingbird feeders are getting dull, please don't waste good nail polish trying to rehabilitate it. Go and get new durable, heavy plastic feeders that are designed for easy filling and cleaning.

6.   Provide snag perches for hummingbirds.

Provide perches near the feeders; hummingbirds use perches to a take break after beating their wings for a rate of 80 beats per second. Hummingbirds like to perch on the edge of expose branches to look out for danger or dive into the air to hunt for insects.

Hummingbirds stay nearby gardens or yards that have a lot of shelter and perches.

Create a snag perch 50 feet from your feeder by sticking a dead branch vertically into the ground.

7. Provide a mister to your yard

Attach a mister in your regular garden hose. A mister's work is to shoot a fine spray or mist into the air through its pinhole openings. Hummingbirds, like all birds, enjoy bathing in moving water or misters by flying through the fine spray until they became soaked. Hummingbird finds it hard to resist that action that comes through mister.

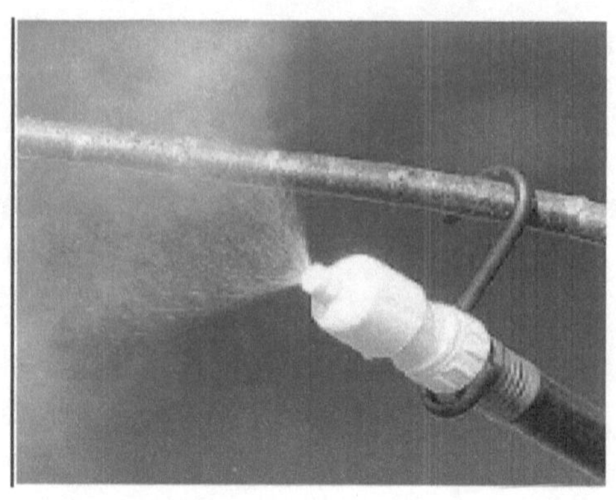

8. Keep hummingbirds Feeders Clean and Fresh

Clean nectar attracts hummingbirds more when it is compared with debris or mold clogged nectar. Clean and refill the hummingbird feeders every few days and ensure all the feeding ports are scrubbed to clear and remove the blockage.

9. Position hummingbird's feeder wisely

If a feeder is not properly placed in a yard, attracting more hummingbirds becomes difficult, no matter how many feeders you have in the garden.

Position a feeder close to an area that has flowers where hummingbirds visit naturally.

Position a feeder close to a perching area or shelters like shrubs or trees.

Position the feeders out of direct sunlight to slow the fermentation process.

Position the feeders where you can see it easily from your house.

Position the feeder in such a way that the reflection of the sunlight coming from the red color and nectar will attract curious hummingbirds prompting them to come and

Make your hummingbirds foods

Nectar Recipes

Medium size feeder

Ingredients

1 cups refined white sugar

4 cups of water

Methods

- In a medium kitchen bowl, add 1 cup of sugar and 4 cups of water.
- Mix thoroughly until the sugar is dissolved.
- Fill your hummingbird feeders with the mixture and place outside.
- Store the extra sugar solution in the refrigerator.
- Clean and refill the feeder every other to prevent mold growth.